PeekSqueak

The Lost Duckling

Dwedor Morais Ford, Ph.D.

DWEDOR MORAIS FORD, PH.D.

Copyright © 2021 by Dwedor Morais Ford, Ph.D.

ISBN   Softcover   978-1-949723-30-4

All rights reserved. No part of this book may be reproduced or transmitted in any form or by any means, electronic or mechanical, including photocopying, recording, or by any information storage and retrieval system without express written permission from the author, except in the case of brief quotations embodied in critical reviews and certain other non-commercial uses permitted by copyright law.

Printed in the United States of America.

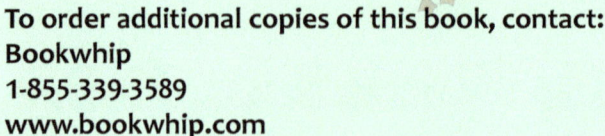

To order additional copies of this book, contact:
Bookwhip
1-855-339-3589
www.bookwhip.com

This book, based on a true story, is dedicated to my grandchildren:

Kailyn, Carrvey, Kwendalyn, Dwedor-Reecie, and Chadow

With Love,
Dowedo

Winh TellingStories, LLC Editorial Staff

Dwedor Morais Ford, Ph.D.	CEO and Editor
Charles Wesley Ford, Jr. Ph.D.	Co-Editor
Charlise Weslea Ford	Co-Editor

I am PeekSqueak, the lost duckling. My mom, eleven siblings, and I live at Shawnee Park in Xenia, Ohio. Because my siblings and I were born at the same time, we are called duodecaplets.

All of my siblings and I look alike, but Mom never gets us mixed up. Mom is the only one who has no trouble identifying each of us.

Our park home is near a busy street. When we go for walks, we cross the street to the other side of the park where the grass is fresh and dry.

One day after our walk, we set out to cross the street to get back home. Humans stopped their cars to let us go safely across the street.

With Mom leading us, one by one we waddled across the road to the other side. Then Mom encouraged us to jump from the bottom of the curb to the grassy area of our park home.

All of my eleven siblings jumped unto the grassy area without much trouble.

I made several attempts to land onto the grass, but on one of my jumps, I fell into the storm drain nearby.

On the grassy area, Mom noticed that I was missing. Upon hearing some familiar sounds, she looked around wondering where the sounds were coming from.

Then she realized that the peeking and squeaking was coming from the storm drain. Before long, she realized it was ME peeking and squeaking.

She flew to the drain and looked in. And there I was at the bottom of the storm drain looking up at her.

She wanted to get me, but she couldn't fit through the grates of the drain. So she quacked loudly!

Humans have fun walking around the park and fishing in the pond. I am glad that two humans, out for a walk in the park that day, saw our family crossing the street. They counted twelve ducklings.

On their way back through the park, they watched my mom going back and forth quacking.

She was trying to keep an eye on her other ducklings while at the same time walking back and forth to the drain to assure me that she was still there.

She got louder every time she neared the drain. The humans wondered what was going on with my mom.

Then they counted:

 one little duckling,

two little ducklings,

three little ducklings,

four little ducklings,

 five little ducklings,

six little ducklings,

seven little ducklings,

eight little ducklings,

nine little ducklings,

ten little ducklings,

eleven little ducklings.

I was LOST!

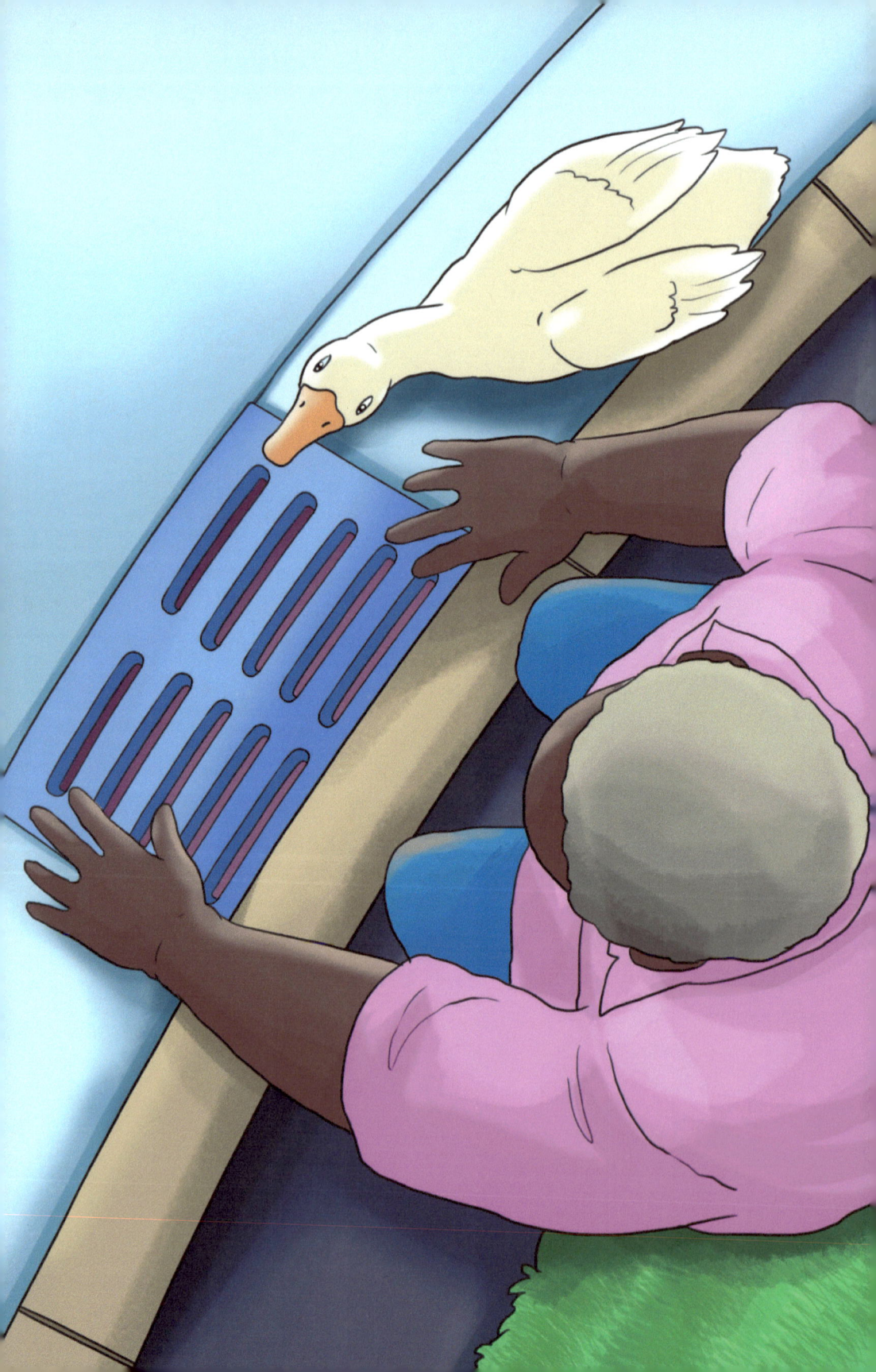

After the humans counted the ducklings, one of the humans looked down the drain and saw me at the bottom.

The humans called the fire department. A firefighter arrived soon after and pulled me out of the drain.

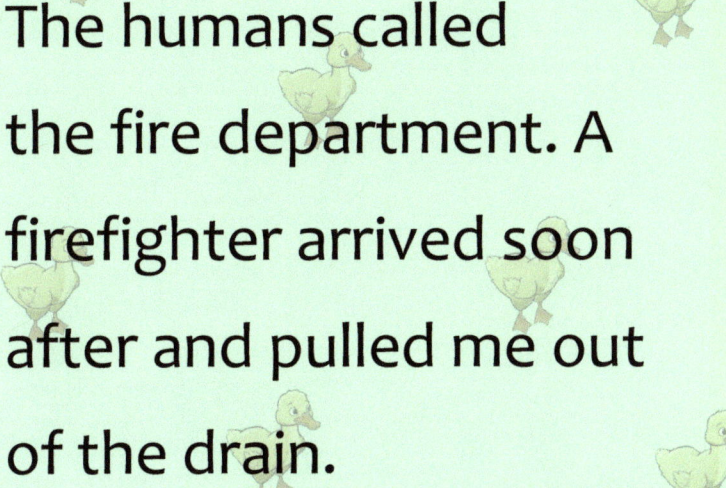

I was happy to be out of that drain and back with my family again. We waddled back to the park where our favorite pond is located.

THE END

www.ingramcontent.com/pod-product-compliance
Lightning Source LLC
Chambersburg PA
CBHW040201100526
44591CB00006B/59